The Sustainable Fashion Business

Launching an Ethical and Eco-Friendly Clothing Brand

Introduction

In a world increasingly aware of its finite resources and responsibilities towards future generations, the need for sustainable and ethical practices spans all aspects of life, including the clothes we wear. Welcome to the revolutionising world of sustainable fashion, where clothing items aren't merely a plaything for vanity but the embodiment of thoughtful purchases that leave a positive imprint on the planet and its inhabitants.

This guide will introduce you to facets of launching your own ethical and eco-friendly fashion brand – a business that merges commerce with a conscience. In an industry often critiqued for its wasteful practices and unsavoury conditions, setting out to make a difference is a remarkable venture, but it indeed comes with its own set of challenges.

How do you strike a balance between style and sustainability? What does it take to craft a product that consumers will adore, and the Earth will appreciate? Where do you start in creating a brand that stands out in a sea of competitors, not merely for its aesthetic appeal but for its Eco-consciousness?

Whether you're an entrepreneur looking to break into the sustainable fashion industry or an existing player hoping to shift towards more ethical practices, this guide will navigate you on the journey to launching an ethical and eco-friendly clothing brand. Together, we will delve into the essences of sustainable fashion, analyse market needs, explore developing an ethical supply chain, discuss effective marketing strategies, and more, ultimately converging to create a brand that leaves its distinct, positive mark on both the business landscape and the world.

Get ready to embark on the path of entrepreneurship that's not just profitable, but also kind to our planet, its people, and its future.

Chapter one

Introduction to Sustainable Fashion Business

1.1 The Concept of Sustainable Fashion

The modern world finds itself in the grips of a consumption cycle that is deceptively dangerous. Our pursuit for the latest fashion trends, often fuelled by a relentless barrage of fast fashion, has accelerated us towards a perilous juncture marked by colossal waste, environmental degradation, and exploitation of workers. But emerging from the shadow of these grim realities is a beacon of change: Sustainable Fashion.

So, what exactly is 'Sustainable Fashion'?

Sustainable Fashion, also known as eco-fashion, refers to clothing that is designed, produced, distributed, and used in ways that are environmentally friendly and socially responsible throughout its entire life cycle. Rather than following the path of 'take, make, and dispose,' sustainable fashion focuses on a more circular economy approach—recycle, repair, refurbish, and repurpose.

Fair labour practices play an integral role in the sustainable fashion conversation. The ethos of sustainable clothing extends beyond just responsible sourcing of materials; it also puts emphasis on how the clothes are made. It whispers a poignant story of wage fairness, workplace safety, empowerment, inclusiveness, and ultimately, dignity for people working across the fashion supply chain.

Sustainable fashion champions a diverse range of elements:

1. Eco-friendly materials: This aspect involves the use of organic fibres and recycled materials that have minimal impact on the environment. The exploration of alternatives, like plant-based dyes, natural fibres, or recycled synthetics, is a significant part of creating a sustainable fibre base.

2. Ethical manufacturing: Ethical manufacturing underscores decent working conditions, fair wages, and safe workplaces for employees in the fashion industry. It's a sphere where respect for human rights isn't a favour bestowed, but a norm adhered to.

3. Slow fashion: Instead of churning out multiple collections a year, sustainable fashion fosters the 'slow fashion' movement that emphasizes timeless

style over fleeting trends, high-quality production over quantity, and long-lasting materials over disposable ones.

4. Transparent Supply Chain: Sustainability leans on transparency, unveiling the journey of a product from inception to completion. It values consumer's rights to know where and under what conditions their clothes are made.

5. Extended Product Lifespan: The drive for sustainability influences not only the creation but the utilization and ultimate disposal of a product. Eco-fashion encourages purchasing less, choosing well, and making items last; it facilitates the repair, resale, or recycling of clothes at the end of their life.

1.2 The Rise of Ethical and Eco-Friendly Brands

In recent years, an increasing number of socially and environmentally conscious consumers have collectively propelled the demand for ethical and eco-friendly fashion. The rise of ethical and eco-friendly brands is the much-needed response to this growing awareness and concern about the dire impact that fast fashion, and its unsustainable business practices, have on our planet and the lives of workers in the fashion industry.

The emergence and rapid growth of ethical and eco-friendly brands can be viewed through various lenses:

1. Consumer Demand for Transparency and Accountability: Consumers today are no longer content with just the end product; they want to know the story behind it. The demand for greater transparency in fashion supply chains has steered

brands towards embracing socially responsible and sustainable manufacturing methods. This rising consumer consciousness has paved the way for fashion brands that prioritize the well-being of both people and the planet.

2. Environmental and Social Media Activism: The power of social media has allowed for the sharing of video, images, and information that reveal the harsh realities of the exploitative practices lurking beneath the glitzy facade of the fashion industry. Activists and influencers have significantly contributed to raising awareness and igniting conversations on responsible fashion. This exposure has provided fertile ground for ethical and eco-friendly brands to establish their presence in the marketplace, as demand shifts towards more sustainable choices.

3. Legislation and Government Initiatives: Government bodies and international organizations have proactively introduced policies, regulations, and initiatives that promote environmentally responsible practices and worker rights. In some countries, ethical and eco-friendly companies often benefit from incentives such as tax breaks or easier access to capital, creating an environment conducive to the establishment and growth of such brands.

4. Collaborative Efforts: Sustainable development often relies on collaborations between brands, suppliers, non-profit organizations, and artisans. Ethical and eco-friendly brands have been successful in fostering partnerships, which create positive social and environmental impact while offering unique and innovative products to consumers.

5. Innovative Solutions and Technology: The rise of ethical and eco-friendly brands can also be attributed to the ever-evolving field of material science and technology. Breakthroughs in developing materials like biodegradable fabrics, plant-based dyes, or innovations like 3D printing and blockchain to track supply chains have provided new means to create and market products that align with and even champion sustainability.

6. Creating Economic Opportunities: Ethical and eco-friendly brands are often lauded for promoting local craftsmanship and fair trade, creating opportunities for underprivileged communities. The dedication to ethical practices and providing stable, proper employment often resonates with consumers and strengthens the appeal of such brands.

Chapter two

Assessing Market Needs

2.1 Understanding Consumer Demand

Understanding consumer demand is a crucial first step in assessing market needs for any business, especially the sustainable fashion business. The preferences, expectations, and purchasing habits of today's consumers have notably shifted towards conscious consumption, ignited by an increasing awareness of the climate crisis, worker exploitation, and the detrimental impacts of fast fashion.

In order to establish effective strategies for a sustainable fashion business, one must delve into the discerning mind of the eco-conscious consumer. Here's how:

1. Identifying the Target Audience: The first aspect lies in identifying who your target consumers are. While the notion of sustainability resonates across various consumer segments, it might be more pronounced in some. For instance, millennials and Gen Z are usually more drawn towards sustainable fashion as they increasingly prioritize environmental and social consciousness.

2. Understanding Purchasing Behaviour: Eco-conscious consumers often favour quality over quantity. They are willing to pay more for sustainable products that promise longevity. Understanding this aspect can guide you in pricing your products and planning your production accordingly.

3. Recognizing Consumer Expectations: The need for transparency is far-reaching among eco-conscious consumers. They value information about the sourcing of materials, production processes, and labour conditions. Understanding this desire for transparency can help shape your communication and marketing strategy.

4. Interpreting Eco-Conscious Values: Sustainable fashion consumers are typically opposed to the planned obsolescence of fast fashion. They are drawn towards timeless designs that transcend seasonal trends. Grasping this can inform your design philosophy and product offerings.

5. Evaluating Consumer Engagement: Consumers today play an active role in advocating for sustainable practices. They want to be associated with brands that are aligned with their values. You can benefit from such consumer engagement by

facilitating platforms for communication, feedback, and collaboration.

6. Market Surveys and Data Analytics: Conducting market surveys and using data analytics tools can provide crucial insights into consumer demand. It helps in gauging the acceptance level of sustainable fashion, identifying trends, and understanding consumer hesitations, if any.

7. Competitor Analysis: Understanding consumer demand also involves studying your competitors in the sustainable fashion market. This could reveal unique selling propositions, gaps in the market, or new opportunities for your brand.

2.2 Identifying Market Opportunities

In the booming realm of sustainable fashion, unique market opportunities are constantly arising. Businesses that accurately identify and seize these opportunities can not only bolster their growth but also contribute significantly to the sustainable fashion movement. Here's a look at some strategic methods to identify market opportunities:

1. Gap Analysis: A gap analysis involves examining the present state of the market and comparing it with its potential state. In the context of sustainable fashion, a gap may exist in providing certain types of attire, servicing specific consumer segments, or operating in certain geographical locations.

2. Consumer Trends and Insights: Keeping a tab on emerging consumer trends and insights is crucial for identifying potential market opportunities. Researching social media platforms, fashion forums, blogs, or conducting surveys can provide such insights. For instance, a rising trend of 'buying local' might provide opportunities for connecting

with local artisans or farmers, thus promoting community sustained businesses.

3. Technological Advancements: The intersection of fashion and technology often paves the way for market opportunities. Capitalizing on eco-innovations such as sustainable fabrics, dyeing methods, 3D printing, or using blockchain to improve transparency in the supply chain can create a competitive advantage for your brand.

4. Collaborations: Collaborations, whether with designers, NGOs, corporates, farmers, or artisans, can open up new markets and opportunities. They can also foster mutual learning and create unique products or collections that appeal to consumers.

5. Regulatory Changes: Staying updated on changes in governmental policies or regulations can also reveal market opportunities. For instance, certain countries may incentivise the use of organic cotton,

which can steer your sourcing choices and potentially lower your production costs.

6. Sustainability Initiatives: Brands that align themselves with larger sustainability goals – such as the United Nations' Sustainable Development Goals – can tap into a broader market scope. This not only escalates brand recognition but also underscores brand values resonating with responsible consumers.

7. Competitive Landscape: Identifying market opportunities also involves an understanding of your competition. Learning from their successes, failures, and strategies can provide crucial insights. It can signal unexplored niche markets, unexpected consumer needs, or areas where your brand could differentiate itself.

Chapter three

Starting your Brand

3.1 Conceptualization of Brand Vision and Mission

Starting a sustainable fashion brand extends well beyond clothing design and production. A key element in the early stages is to conceptualize a clear brand vision and mission. These guiding principles serve as the compass that steer your brand direction, inform your operations, and help build an authentic connection with your audience.

Vision

Your brand vision is essentially the aspiration you have for your company's future. It encapsulates where you see your brand in years to come in the realm of sustainable fashion.

A clear vision takes into consideration:

1. Purpose: Your brand vision should reflect the broader purpose of your company beyond just monetary gain. As a sustainable fashion brand, your purpose might be to contribute to environmentally-friendly practices, promote ethically sourced materials, or uplift artisan communities.

2. Impact: The vision should hint at the projected impact your brand seeks to make - environmentally, socially, or even within the industry itself. For instance, your vision could be to drastically reduce the fashion industry's carbon footprint.

3. Identity: A strong vision articulates the brand identity you aim to foster. This includes the lasting

impression your brand seeks to leave in the minds of customers and industry stakeholders.

Mission

Your brand mission is the actionable path to achieve the envisioned future - the "how". It outlines the strategy, methods, and values that you intend to use to fulfill your vision.

Here's what a well-defined mission takes into account:

1. Manifestation of Values: Your brand mission should effectively communicate the core values driving your operations. It should express your commitment to sustainability, how you aim to uphold it, and the ethics guiding your business decisions.

2. Engage the Audience: The mission should engage the audience by highlighting how your brand will meet their needs or address their concerns. For

instance, you might commit to offering ethically made, high-quality, timeless pieces.

3. Stakeholder Relations: The mission should also briefly touch upon how you intend to foster relationships with various stakeholders (e.g., suppliers, employees, shareholders, or artisan communities).

3.2 Defining Your Unique Value Proposition

Creating a sustainable fashion brand in an increasingly competitive market requires a well-defined unique value proposition (UVP). Your UVP is the element that sets your brand apart from the competition and communicates the distinct benefit, value, or experience customers can expect from your products.

Here are some steps to take when defining your unique value proposition for your sustainable fashion brand:

1. Identify Your Target Customer

Clearly define your target customer by considering demographics, buying habits, preferences, and the definition of sustainability they resonate with the most. This allows you to direct your value proposition towards the specific needs and desires of your ideal customer.

2. Understand Your Competition

Evaluate your competitors in the sustainable fashion market and analyze their value propositions. Identify any gaps, areas they excel in, and areas where they fall short. This can provide insights into opportunities for differentiating your brand.

3. Rely on Your Strengths

Your UVP should emphasize the unique strengths of your brand, merging them with the needs of your target market. Perhaps your brand uses innovative technologies in sustainable fabric production, collaborates with renowned eco-conscious designers, or supports local artisans and craftsmanship. Emphasize these strengths and translate them into the value your customers can expect.

4. Hone Your Sustainability Narrative

Sustainable fashion brands often have powerful sustainability narratives that resonate with the customer's values and emotions. Identify which aspect of sustainability plays a starring role in your brand story and incorporate it into your UVP. This might include a focus on zero waste, fair labor practices, or eco-friendly packaging.

5. Test and Iterate

Present your UVP drafts to focus groups or run marketing tests to gather feedback. Refine the most resonating UVP and continue iterating as your brand grows or as you receive more feedback from customers.

6. Consistency Is Key

Your UVP should be consistent across all communication channels, such as your website, social media, and marketing materials. Ensure that your team is aligned with the UVP, and it is ingrained in your brand culture.

Chapter four
Creating an Ethical Supply Chain

4.1 Sourcing Sustainable Materials

Building a reliable, ethical, and sustainable supply chain is a central tenet of a sustainable fashion brand. Sourcing sustainable materials is among the first steps in this process. The materials you choose can have significant implications on your brand's environmental footprint and the quality and longevity of your products.

Here are a few strategies to consider while sourcing sustainable materials:

1. Understand Different Types of Sustainable Materials

Understanding the composition and impact of various sustainable materials is critical. Some commonly used materials include:

- Organic Cotton: Organic cotton is grown without harmful synthetic chemicals and is often more robust than conventional cotton.

- Bamboo, Hemp, and Linen: These fast-growing plants require less water and pesticides than conventional crops. They also can be produced sustainably and turned into durable fabrics.

- Recycled and Upcycled Materials: Using recycled or upcycled materials not only reduces landfill waste, but also minimizes the need for new material production.

- Innovative Materials: These include lab-grown leather, bio-based textiles, or fabrics made from recycled plastic bottles.

2. Establish Relationships with Suppliers

Building a relationship with ethical suppliers and manufacturers that align with your sustainability values and commitments is crucial. Visit production sites, know their practices, and ensure they share your vision of sustainability.

3. Consider Availability, Cost, and Quality

The sustainably sourced material should be readily available, affordable, and of high quality. Sometimes, the cost of sustainable materials can be higher compared with conventional options, but this can be offset by the longer durability of your products and the willingness of eco-conscious customers to pay a premium for sustainably-made items.

4. Certifications and Standards

Verify the authenticity of your materials by checking for certifications such as the Global Organic Textile Standard (GOTS) or the STANDARD 100 by OEKO-TEX®. Recognized certifications can provide assurance to your customers about your sustainability commitments.

5. Close-loop Production

Aim for a close-loop production cycle where waste from one process becomes the raw material for another. This helps in creating an integrated, waste-free supply chain.

6. Transparent Sourcing

Transparency in sourcing is appreciated by conscious consumers. Share information about where and how your materials are sourced to build trust and authenticate your brand's sustainability claims.

4.2 Collaborating with Ethical Manufacturers

To thrive as a sustainable fashion brand, it is crucial that your ethical commitments extend throughout your entire supply chain. A key aspect of this mission is partnering with ethical manufacturers who share similar values and contribute to the creation of an end-to-end ethical supply chain.

Here are some factors to consider when collaborating with ethical manufacturers:

1. Prioritize Fair Labor Practices

Your chosen manufacturer should prioritize fair labor practices, ensuring workers receive:

- Fair wages, meeting or exceeding industry standards and local regulations.

- A safe and healthy working environment, with compliance to industry norms like safety gear and regular safety assessments.

- Reasonable working hours and time off, in alignment with labor laws and industry standards.

- Freedom from discrimination, exploitation, and child labor.

2. Focus on Environmental Stewardship

The manufacturer should adhere to eco-friendly practices such as:

- Minimizing pollution through responsible waste management and emissions control.

- Employing sustainable practices like water recycling, reduced energy usage, and renewable energy sources.

- Prioritizing the use of eco-friendly raw materials and chemicals.

3. Evaluate Expertise and Quality

Partner with manufacturers that have experience and expertise in working with sustainable materials and production processes to ensure high-quality products. Their commitment to quality should be evident through their track record, customer feedback, and accreditations.

4. Check for Certifications and Compliance

Assess the manufacturer's certifications, such as B Corp, Fair Wear Foundation, Worldwide Responsible Accredited Production (WRAP), or ISO 14001. These certifications can validate the manufacturer's adherence to social and environmental standards.

5. Build Long-term Partnerships

Collaborate with manufacturers that you can build long-term relationships with, ensuring a consistent supply of ethically produced, high-quality products. This can help your brand minimise its environmental impact by reducing transportation-related emissions and streamlining operations.

6. Foster Open Communication

Establish open communication channels with your manufacturers to discuss improvements, address concerns, and report on progress. This will create a positive work environment, build trust, and ensure the manufacturer understands and aligns with your brand's values.

7. Strive for Supply Chain Transparency

Transparency fosters consumer trust and accountability. Provide customers information about the manufacturing process, including the partners you work with, production locations, and labour practices. This practice will authenticate your brand's commitment to ethical

production.

Chapter five
Designing your Product Line

5.1 Prioritizing Quality Over Quantity

Quality over quantity is a widely embraced philosophy in the sustainable fashion industry. The principle encourages brands to focus on creating long-lasting, versatile pieces rather than indulging in mass production that inevitably leads to excessive consumption. By producing thoughtfully designed, durable garments, your brand not only minimizes environmental impact but also fosters a more sustainable relationship with customers.

Here are some strategies on prioritising quality over quantity when designing your product line:

1. Timeless Design

Instead of following short-lived trends, create classic styles and timeless designs that remain relevant for years. This enables customers to wear your garments for extended periods and reduces the need for frequent wardrobe updates.

2. Durable Materials

Select high-quality, sustainable materials that withstand wear and tear and retain their shape, colour, and texture over time. By prioritizing durability, you are actively reducing the rate of consumption and waste.

3. Impeccable Craftsmanship

Invest in skilled artisans and manufacturers who produce well-constructed garments. Pay close attention to details such as stitching, seam allowances, and finishing.

High-quality craftsmanship not only extends the life of your products but also reinforces your brand's reputation for excellence.

4. Versatile Design

Create garments that can be worn in multiple ways or serve various functions. Versatile, multi-use products help consumers build a more flexible, minimalist wardrobe and discourage excessive consumption.

5. Educate Your Customers

Encourage your customer base to adopt quality-focused buying habits by promoting the value of investing in durable, well-crafted garments. Share tips on proper garment care and maintenance to help customers prolong the life of their purchases.

6. Foster Loyalty Through Sustainability

Build a loyal customer base by rewarding their sustainable choices and behaviors. Offer repair services, incentivize recycling, and promote sustainable garment care options such as eco-friendly detergents and energy-saving laundry practices.

7. Small Batch Production

Consider producing garments in small batches to minimize overstock and waste. This approach allows you to maintain quality control whilst being responsive to demand and minimizing the harm to the environment.

8. Opt for a Seasonless Approach

Free your brand from the constraints of seasonal collections by adopting a seasonless approach. Create designs with timeless appeal and better equipped to withstand changing trends, encouraging longer-lasting relationships between customers and your products.

5.2 Incorporating Upcycling and Recycling In Design

Incorporating upcycling and recycling in your design process is a potent strategy in sustainable fashion, resulting in an exciting and innovative product line. By repurposing discarded materials or transforming waste into valuable resources, you can significantly decrease your brand's environmental impact while offering unique, eco-conscious products.

Here are some steps to help you incorporate upcycling and recycling in your design process:

1. Sourcing Materials

Start collecting and sourcing materials that can be upcycled or recycled. This might include waste textiles from your own production, fabric scraps from other businesses, or even used garments from customers. Be creative and open-minded about the potential of these 'waste' materials.

2. Prioritize Quality

Ensure that the collection and sorting processes focus on quality. For upcycled items, fabrics should still be in good condition and suitable for the intended end use. For recycled fabrics, the process should be able to break down materials safely and efficiently.

3. Design with Upcycling and Recycling in Mind

Design your products to be conducive to future upcycling or recycling. Consider factors like ease of disassembly, mix of materials, and potential for repurposing elements when the product reaches the end of its life cycle.

4. Partner with Ethical Manufacturers

Search for manufacturers who specialize in upcycled or recycled products. They will be equipped with the necessary skills and machinery to ensure the quality of your products, and they will likely share your sustainability values.

5. Develop Upcycling Programs

Think about setting up programs that enable and incentivize your customers to upcycle or recycle their old garments. This could include trade-in schemes, recycling programs, or DIY upcycling workshops.

6. Communicate the Value of Upcycling and Recycling

Educate your audience about the benefits of upcycled and recycled fashion. Illustrate the uniqueness of each piece, the story behind it, and the environmental impact of their purchase. This will help foster a deeper connection between your customers and your products.

7. Validate Products with Certifications

Seek relevant certifications such as the Global Recycled Standard (GRS), Recycled Claim Standard (RCS), or Upcycled Certified™ to provide assurance to your customers about the validity of your claims and to increase transparency and credibility.

Chapter six

Marketing Your Brand

6.1 Establishing A Transparent Marketing Strategy

In an era where consumers are growing more conscious and cognizant of their purchasing power, transparency has become a critical ingredient in the success recipe of sustainable fashion brands. Establishing a transparent marketing strategy enables your brand to build trust, foster customer loyalty, and highlight your commitment to ethical practices and sustainability.

Here are some strategies to build transparency into your marketing efforts:

1. Share your Values and Mission

Clearly articulate your brand's values and mission in all your communications, including your website, social media, and product packaging. Let your audience know what your brand stands for and how you aim to contribute to a more sustainable future.

2. Provide Clarity on your Supply Chain

Be open about your supply chain, from raw materials sourcing to product manufacturing. Share insights about your partners, the countries where your products are made, and the fair practices you uphold to ensure employee welfare.

3. Detail your Sustainability Efforts

Provide specific, measurable details about your sustainability initiatives. Whether it's reducing carbon emissions, implementing water-saving practices, or using recycled materials, offer quantifiable proof to substantiate your claims.

4. Showcase Certifications, Accreditations and Partnerships

Highlight any certifications, accreditations, or partnerships you have achieved or established that support your sustainability claims. This could include certifications like Global Organic Textile Standard (GOTS), Fairtrade, or Worldwide Responsible Accredited Production (WRAP) among others.

5. Humanize your Brand

Tell the stories of the people behind your brand. From designers and artisans to factory workers, share their narratives to project a human face, fostering a deeper connection with your audience.

6. Engage with your Audience

Be open and responsive to enquiries and feedback. Establish various channels (social media, email, customer service lines) to facilitate effective two-way communication.

7. Educate your Customers

Take on the role of an educator. Share educational content related to sustainable fashion and the impact of consumption habits. This fosters informed decision-making, offers value to your audience, and positions your brand as an authority in the field.

8. Promote Transparency in Pricing

Offer detailed explanations of your product pricing, breaking down costs associated with production, labour, shipping, and other factors. This will provide your clients with an understanding of where their money is going and why sustainable fashion can often be more expensive.

6.2 Leveraging Social Media for Brand Awareness

In today's digital age, social media serves as a highly effective tool for marketing your sustainable fashion brand. Not only can it significantly improve your brand visibility, but also provide opportunities to engage with your audience directly, driving deeper connections and fostering a loyal customer base. Here's how you can leverage social media for brand awareness:

1. Understand Your Target Audience
Understanding your audience is paramount to effectively use social media. Research who your ideal customers are, their values, and the social platforms they are most active on. Essentially, your target audience should align with your brand's values and appreciate your sustainable efforts.

2. Curate Visual Narratives

Visual content, especially high-quality images, infographics, and videos, attract more engagement than text-based posts. Use these mediums to convey your sustainable initiatives, brand story, and behind-the-scenes looks at the production process.

3. Humanize Your Brand

People connect with people, not faceless entities. Showcase team members, designers, artisans, and even your customers. Tell their stories to bring a human touch to your brand and foster emotional connections.

4. Engage through Authentic Content

Emphasize honesty, authenticity, and transparency in your posts. Discuss your sustainability goals, the challenges you face, and the steps you are taking to overcome them.

Authenticity breeds trust, which plays a crucial role in customer loyalty and brand reputation.

5. Use Relevant Hashtags

Hashtags are a powerful tool to increase your post visibility. Use popular, relevant hashtags that correspond with your brand, such as #SustainableFashion, #EthicalFashion, #ZeroWaste, etc. But also consider creating unique branded hashtags to foster a community around your brand.

6. Collaborate and Partner

Consider partnering with influencers, other brands, or even NGOs that align with your brand's values. Joint initiatives could range from influencer takeovers, shout-outs, contests, or even product collaborations.

7. Encourage User-Generated Content

Invite customers to share photos of them wearing your items, providing reviews, or even how they are leading a sustainable lifestyle. User-generated content is a powerful endorsement of your products and fosters community.

8. Stay Active and Consistent

Make sure you post regularly on your social media channels, and maintain the same tone and style. Regular posts will keep your audience interested, while consistency ensures your brand message remains cohesive.

9. Listen, Respond, and Engage

Engage with your followers regularly. Respond to comments, take on board feedback, and show appreciation for their input. This level of interaction strengthens your relationship with your audience, encouraging brand loyalty.

Chapter seven
Sales and Distribution

7.1 Selecting Sustainable Packaging

As a sustainable fashion brand, it is essential to consider every aspect of your business, including packaging, sales, and distribution. Choosing sustainable packaging alternatives demonstrates your commitment to eco-friendly practices, reduces waste, and adds value for environmentally conscious customers.

Here are some factors to consider when selecting sustainable packaging for your sales and distribution process:

1. Materials

Undoubtedly, materials are a crucial aspect of sustainable packaging. Consider biodegradable, recycled, or compostable materials to minimize environmental impact. Examples of sustainable materials include:

- Recycled or FSC-certified paper and cardboard

- Biodegradable or compostable mailers

- Plant-based packaging materials (e.g., cornstarch-based bioplastics)

2. Size and Weight

Packaging size should be designed to fit the product snugly, eliminating the need for excess packing and reducing overall material utilization. Lightweight packaging reduces shipping costs and has a lower environmental impact due to decreased transportation emissions.

3. Reusability

Provide packaging that can be repurposed or reused by your customers. Encourage reusability by offering incentives, ideas, or discounts for customers who return packaging materials or share creative upcycling solutions.

4. Logistics and Supply Chain

Partner with suppliers and manufacturers that prioritize sustainable practices. Source your packaging materials locally when possible to reduce transport emissions and support local businesses.

5. Ink and Printing

Opt for eco-friendly inks, such as water-based, soy-based, or vegetable-based inks, which have lower VOC emissions and are less harmful to the environment. Additionally, minimize printing on packaging to further reduce emissions.

6. Packaging Lifecycle

Evaluate the lifecycle of your packaging materials and assess their end-of-life impact. Choose materials that can be either recycled (without compromising quality), composted, or biodegraded easily.

7. Customer Education

Highlight your sustainable packaging choices by providing information to customers about the materials used and how they can properly dispose of them. This helps foster eco-conscious behaviour and increases the likelihood of proper recycling or composting.

8. Carbon Offsetting and Certifications

Consider joining carbon offset programs or certification systems like Climate Neutral, which allow you to measure, reduce, and offset your packaging's carbon footprint.

Promote these certifications on your packaging to make an impression on eco-conscious customers.

9. Critique and Adjust

Regularly review your packaging strategy to ensure that it is up to date with industry advancements, addresses issues, and continuously improves its sustainability performance.

7.2 Choosing Eco-Friendly Distribution Channels

As a sustainable fashion brand, it is essential to consider the environmental impact of your distribution strategy. Selecting eco-friendly distribution channels helps to ensure you are minimizing your carbon footprint while maintaining efficient and reliable product delivery. Here are key considerations in choosing environmentally conscious distribution channels for your business:

1. Opt for Local and Regional Shipping Companies

Support local and regional shipping companies, considering they are more familiar with the area and its resources. Some local distributors may use sustainable practices, such as electric or hybrid vehicles, and are frequently more cost-effective due to their familiarity with the region.

2. Collaborative Shipping and Distribution

Partner with other sustainable fashion brands or companies to consolidate shipments. This approach reduces packaging requirements, shipping costs, and transportation emissions, while enabling you to optimize distribution logistics.

3. Low-Emission Vehicles

Partner with shipping companies that prioritize low-emission vehicles like electric or hybrid fleets. These partnerships help reduce harmful transportation emissions and bolster your brand's commitment to sustainability.

4. Bulk Packaging and Delivery

If feasible, negotiate with retailers or stockists to accept bulk packaging deliveries instead of individually packaged items. This strategy not only minimizes the need for packaging materials but also reduces transportation emissions.

5. Efficient Route Planning

Efficient route planning is vital in minimizing carbon emissions. Request that your shipping partner optimize and plan routes to reduce distances, fuel consumption, and emissions.

6. Sustainable Warehouse and Storage Facilities

Partner with warehouse and storage facilities that prioritize eco-friendly practices, such as energy-efficient lighting, waste reduction, and recycling. These partnerships can decrease the environmental impact of your supply chain infrastructure.

7. Investigate Last-Mile Delivery Solutions

Explore innovative last-mile delivery solutions like local drop-off points, bicycle couriers, or collaborations with zero-emission vehicle companies. These services reduce the environmental impact of the final stage in your product's journey to the customer.

8. Carbon Offsetting Programs

Many shipping companies offer carbon offsetting programs, which allow you to estimate and offset your yearly shipping emissions. By participating in such programs, you can balance out your distribution impact by investing in eco-friendly projects or initiatives.

9. Communicate Your Practices

Inform customers about your eco-friendly distribution methods, either on your website, social media, or packaging. Transparency and communication strengthen customer loyalty and showcase your brand's commitment to sustainability.

10. Continuously Evaluate and Improve

Regularly review and assess your distribution channels for any inefficiencies or areas for improvement. Advancements in technology, new partnerships, or updated regulations may offer opportunities to further optimize distribution and minimize environmental impact.

Chapter eight

After Sales Service and Consumer Education

8.1 Implementing A Sustainable Returns Policy

The ease of online returns has led to a significant increase in reverse logistics. However, this process can have substantial environmental impacts, from carbon emissions due to transportation to waste generated from non-resellable products. For a sustainable fashion brand, creating an eco-friendly returns policy is crucial, requiring careful balancing between commercial feasibility, customer satisfaction, and environmental impact.

Below are key aspects to consider when creating a sustainable returns policy:

1. Limit Unnecessary Returns

Encourage customers to make mindful purchases by providing detailed product information (measurements, materials, fit, etc.), high-quality product images, and even virtual try-on tools. This minimizes the chance of customers buying multiple items to try on at home and returning the rest.

2. Extended Returns Window

Offer an extended return timeframe, which can encourage customers to return items via slower, more sustainable shipping methods.

3. Encourage Store Returns

Promote in-store returns, where feasible. This approach reduces shipping impacts and adds an opportunity for your staff to build face-to-face relationships with customers.

4. Efficient Packaging for Returns

Design packaging that can be easily reused for returns. This not only reduces the demand for new return packaging but also simplifies the return process for consumers.

5. Repurpose Returned Goods

If items cannot be resold, look for alternatives to maximize their life - donate, recycle or upcycle them, or partner with organizations that can give them a second life.

6. Discount for Sustainable Shipping

Offer a small discount or incentive for customers who choose a sustainable return shipping option, such as slower delivery times or grouped returns.

7. Digital Receipts and Return Labels

Encourage digital receipts and return labels to minimize paper usage. By doing this, you also provide members the convenience of easy access to their purchase or return information at any time.

8. Implement Buy-Back or Trade-In Programs

Consider implementing a buy-back or trade-in program where customers can return used items for a discount on their next purchase. This keeps products in a circular loop and reduces waste.

9. Educate Consumers

Educate your customers about the environmental impact of returns and how they can make sustainable choices. Encourage them to consolidate returns, return in person where possible, and think critically about their purchase decisions.

10. Regular Policy Review

Regularly review and adapt your returns policy keeping in mind the dynamic nature of the consumer market and sustainable practices.

8.2 Educating Consumers On Sustainable Fashion

In a market where consumers are increasingly aware and conscious of the effect their purchases have on the environment, providing education about sustainable fashion becomes a critical part of running a green fashion brand.

Here's how to successfully engage and educate consumers about sustainable fashion practices:

1. Storytelling

Use storytelling to share information about the impact of the fashion industry on the environment and how your brand is implementing changes for a greener future. Authentic, compelling stories can help consumers connect with your brand and its values on a deeper level.

2. Product Information

Provide detailed product information - from the material used to the manufacturing process. Transparency fosters trust and enables consumers to understand the impact of their purchases.

3. Workshops and Seminars

Host interactive workshops or seminars to educate customers on various aspects of sustainable fashion. Topics might include recycling old clothing, making sustainable clothing choices, or caring for garments to extend their life.

4. Social Media, Blogs, and Newsletters

Spread your message using digital platforms. Regularly update your company blog, social media channels, and newsletters with articles, infographics, and video content related to sustainable fashion.

5. Collaborate with Influencers

Work with influencers who are passionate about sustainability. They can help spread your brand's message, and their support can provide credibility to your sustainability efforts and reach a broader audience.

6. Sustainability Policies and Initiatives

Clearly articulate and communicate your sustainability policies, initiatives, and achievements. Highlight any carbon-offset programs, partnerships with sustainable suppliers, or other endeavors that reduce your brand's environmental footprint.

7. Encourage Consumer Input

Encourage feedback and suggestions from your customers. This interactive dialogue can enhance consumer education and make your customers feel more involved in your sustainability journey.

8. Responsible Care Instructions

Provide responsible care instructions for your garments, such as cold wash, air dry, mending tips, or even suggestions for recycling or upcycling once the item has reached the end of its wearable life.

9. In-Store Information

Incorporate educational materials and signage around your retail store to inform and engage shoppers about sustainable fashion. This could include information about the materials used in your items, stats about the environmental impact of the fashion industry, or details about your brand's sustainability initiatives.

10. Sustainability Training for Staff

Empower your staff with knowledge about sustainable fashion, so they can educate and answer customer queries efficiently. Well-informed employees can serve as enthusiastic ambassadors for your brand and its

sustainability values.

Chapter nine

Review and Plan for Future

9.1 Evaluation of Business Performance

Evaluating your sustainable fashion brand's performance is essential for identifying areas of improvement, implementing new strategies, and evolving with industry trends. Routinely assessing and adapting your business operations ensures long-term success, growth, and sustainability.

Below are key aspects to consider when reviewing your business performance:

1. Sales Data

Analyze sales data, consumer preferences, and purchasing patterns to identify which products are performing well, seasonality trends, and insights into target markets. This enables you to make informed decisions about inventory management, product development, and marketing strategies.

2. Environmental Impact Analysis

Evaluate your brand's environmental impact with factors like energy consumption, water usage, and carbon emissions. Identify opportunities to reduce waste, improve efficiency, and optimize resource management across your supply chain.

3. Social Responsibility and Ethics

Assess your brand's social responsibility and ethical performance, considering factors like fair labour practices, employee satisfaction, and community engagement. Create or adapt initiatives that strengthen these aspects, ensuring your brand remains reputable and responsible.

4. Sustainability Goals and Benchmarks

Set clear sustainability goals and industry-aligned benchmarks, such as reduced energy consumption, increased use of renewable materials, or zero waste production. Regularly track and assess progress toward these goals to gauge the success of your sustainability efforts.

5. Customer Satisfaction and Feedback

Review customer feedback, engagement rates, and purchasing behaviours to improve customer satisfaction and understand their preferences. Communication and collaboration with your customers are invaluable to ensure your brand's continuous improvement.

6. Market Position

Analyze your brand's position in the market concerning key competitors. Examine their strengths and weaknesses to identify areas where you can enhance your own brand visibility, competitive edge, and unique selling proposition.

7. Financial Performance

Evaluate financial performance by analyzing revenue, profits, operating costs, and budget allocations. Efficient financial management supports long-term growth and sustainability.

8. Employee Performance and Satisfaction

Monitor employee satisfaction and performance, identifying areas for improvement, development, or training. Engaged and satisfied employees contribute to productivity and increased success.

9. Marketing and Advertising Efforts

Review the effectiveness of your marketing and advertising efforts, assessing metrics such as reach, impressions, conversions, and return on investment (ROI). Identify the best performing channels and strategies to optimize future campaigns.

10. Innovation and Adaptability

Continually research new technologies, innovations, and industry trends to ensure your brand remains adaptable, up-to-date, and resilient.

9.2 Planning for Future Growth and Expansions

Sustainable growth and expansion are vital components of successful fashion businesses. Equally important is factoring in sustainability goals and core values in the growth plan. Here are essential steps to plan for future growth and expansion within the sustainable fashion industry:

1. Define Your Vision and Mission

Your brand's vision and mission provide a roadmap for future growth and serve as a guide when making strategic decisions. Clearly articulate your brand's long-term aspirations and how you plan to maintain your sustainability commitments.

2. Market Research

Conduct thorough market research to identify potential markets, consumer preferences, unique opportunities, and market trends. Research competitors and examine their strengths, weaknesses, and growth strategies to make informed decisions about your expansion plans.

3. Set Long-Term Goals and Objectives

Define long-term growth and sustainability objectives that align with your brand values and mission. Break these goals down into actionable steps and viable timelines, ensuring both growth and sustainability goals are met.

4. Develop a Strategy for Expansion

Design a comprehensive expansion strategy that considers new markets, diversification of products, collaboration opportunities, and scaling up of production. Assess production facilities, logistical considerations, and the financial viability of each expansion plan.

5. Prioritize Sustainability in Expansion Plans

Ensure that your growth plans incorporate sustainable practices, from material sourcing to production processes, waste management, and green logistics. Expansion should not compromise the core sustainability principles of your business.

6. Secure Funding

Identify and secure the necessary funding for expansion through investors, grants, loans, or crowdfunding. Ensure that potential investors and partners align with your brand's ethical and sustainability values.

7. Evaluate Human Resource Needs

Determine future staffing needs to support growth and expansion. Invest in employee training and development to build a skilled workforce that is dedicated to your brand's growth and sustainability objectives.

8. Scale-Up Operations

Develop a plan to scale up operations and logistics without compromising on sustainability or quality. Collaborate with like-minded suppliers and production facilities to maintain your brand's ethical practices at an expanded scale.

9. Implement New Technologies

Embrace new technologies and innovative solutions that help streamline production, reduce waste, and improve efficiency. This could include integrating renewable energy sources, adopting circular fashion practices, or utilizing technology for material innovation.

10. Monitor Progress and Adjust

Continually reassess your growth plans and progress toward your objectives. Adjust strategies based on market and industry changes, and address any areas that need improvement.

Conclusion

In conclusion, launching an ethical and eco-friendly clothing brand in today's fashion landscape necessitates a firm commitment to sustainability both in practice and ethos. This journey, though challenging, is a powerful response to the fashion industry's environmental impact and consumers' increasing demand for more responsible options.

The initiation phase requires thorough planning - from identifying your target market and formulating a unique selling proposition to developing a sustainable business model and sourcing ethical suppliers. This preliminary ground-work is critical for establishing a solid foundation for the brand.

Product design and development also play integral roles, requiring a careful and innovative approach to incorporate eco-friendly materials, ethical manufacturing processes, and designs that promote longevity and recyclability.

As the brand grows, constant evaluation of business performance is imperative for identifying successes, understanding areas for improvement, and planning for future growth. Here, reviewing sales data, environmental impact, financial performance, and customer satisfaction, among others, helps maintain continuous development.

In preparing for the future, sustainable growth and expansion planning are key. This involves setting long-term goals, developing an expansion strategy, securing funding, and scaling operations, all while upholding sustainability principles at the core of every decision.

Marketing and consumer education are other irreplaceable aspects. From creating compelling storytelling and providing detailed product information to using digital platforms for spreading the message, brands can effectively reach and educate consumers about sustainable fashion. Encouraging consumer input, training staff on sustainability, and collaborating with influencers also helps drive engagement and brand loyalty.

The journey to launching and running a sustainable fashion brand is not easy. It requires determination, passion, and a deep commitment to sustainable change. However, the rewards are worth the effort. Businesses will not only be profitable but also contribute to creating a more sustainable and ethical fashion industry. Such brands don't just sell products; they create a movement, inspire change, and play a fundamental role in sculpting a healthier planet for current and future generations.

In the fast-paced, ever-evolving fashion world, it's those brands that choose to stand for something more significant than just fashion trends who truly make a lasting impact. A sustainable fashion business, in essence, represents an inspiring fusion of style and sustainability—a powerful stride toward a more sustainable and socially responsible world.